CW00362448

Celebrity Limericks

Ridiculous Rhymes
about the Rich and Famous

To Ken

Thank you for your
sterling work on our
accounts.

Helen M. Grant.

CELEBRITY LIMERICKS

Ridiculous Rhymes
about the Rich and Famous

by

Helen M. Grant

Over the Ramparts Publishing

Text © Helen M. Grant 2007

Illustrations © Over the Ramparts Publishing, with thanks
to Tony Hinwood of The Hinwood Library of Ideas

First published in Great Britain 2007
by Over the Ramparts Publishing
an imprint of Broomfield Books Limited
36 De La Warr Road, East Grinstead
West Sussex RH19 3BP

A CIP catalogue record for this title is available from the
British Library.

ISBN 978-1-906375-00-3

Typeset in Goudy Old Style
By www.wilsondesign.org

Printed and bound in the United Kingdom
By Mackays of Chatham plc

For my father,
John Leslie

There was a man born in Jalpaiguri
Whose dad ran a plantation of tea
Second World War soldier
Concorde brakes' designer
This book's dedicated to John Leslie!

CONTENTS

CONTENTS

MAGNIFICENT MUSICIANS

Born in Melbourne, diminutive Kylie
Neighbours' star – She Should be so Lucky
Better the Devil You Know
Spinning Around, take it Slow
Showgirl, Impossible Princess, Aussie!

A Material Girl from the Bay City
Madonna Louise Veronica Ciccone
From Virgin to Evita
And Vogue to Erotica
Desperately Seeking Mrs Guy Ritchie!

From Louisiana Britney Spears
When young was one of the Mouseketeers
Hit her Baby One More Time
Or Oops She'll Do It Again
And cut off her hair with the shears!

A baritone born in Glasgow in Scotland
Joseph and Maria Judge, John Barrowman
Star of Anything Goes
Miss Saigon, other shows
Starred in Torchwood as Jack Harkness, Captain!

A certain Reg Dwight born in Pinner
Became Elton John, the pop singer
Daniel and Song for Guy
Yellowbrick Road – Goodbye
Still Standing - a compulsive shopper!

Voice of an Angel, of Welsh extraction
She's going out with Gavin Henson
Pie Jesu, the first hit
For Charlotte Church, Crazy Chick
George Bush asked her what country Wales was in!

A great singer raised in Hertfordshire
He's Your Man for a Careless Whisper
Faith, Freedom and Wham!
An L. A. Policeman
Arrested him for lewd behaviour!

A great mover born in Memphis, Tennessee
Justin Timberlake was in the MMC
*NSYNC performer
Cry Me a River
Justified going solo – won a Grammy!

A Soul and Jazz singer from Southgate
Amy Winehouse, being Frank, was in a state
Back to Black she'd gone
Now she's so Strong
Gone to Rehab, so it's not too late.

Born in Indiana's City of Gary
He's the Man in the Mirror, "Hee Hee"
His moonwalk's a winner
His life is a Thriller
Just Off the Wall or is he History?

A performer born in Stoke-on-Trent
Robbie Williams from Take That! he went
He swings when he's winning
The Rock DJ's singing
The success of Angels was heaven sent!

A singer born in Highgate, London
He loves his football and wears tartan
His voice is all gravely
Do You Think He's Sexy?
Rod Stewart's got married again!

High-pitched rasper born in Wallsend
Message in a Bottle to send
Don't Stand So Close to Me
In Synchronicity
Howay, The Police have reformed!

Victoria born in Hertfordshire
Held her designer labels so dear
Also known as Posh Spice
Left 'Beckingham Palace'
For Hollywood, but is that Girl Power?

BIG ON THE BOX

From London, entertainer Bruce Forsyth
Didn't he do well? He Played his Cards Right!
Oh, he had a twirl
Then married Miss World
Strictly, Nice to see you, to see you nice!

That Antony Cotton born in Bury
He plays Coronation Street's Sean Tully
Won Soapstar Superstar
Soap Awards Best Actor
Now he has his own show on the telly!

There was a high-pitched lady from Brixton
Star of The Osbournes, red-haired Sharon
Wed the Prince of Darkness
And due to her frankness
Extreme, bio of the year, sold two million!

An actor from Ilkeston, Derbyshire
Captain in the Royal Welsh Fusiliers
William Roache's alter ego
Coronation Street's Ken Barlow
Goes to the Rovers Return for his beers!

A development guru from Reading
Constant hair changes, always expecting
Had her Beeny babies
Bossy with her trainees
Property Ladder – Sarah's still climbing!

From Brighton, Mr Nasty, Simon Cowell
Made his name as a judge on Pop Idol
Was mail boy at EMI
He wears his trousers high
"I Don't Mean to be Rude, But..." with a scowl!

A sharp satirist born in Swansea
Appears in the courts regularly
The News He's Got for You
In Private Eye is true
Ian Hislop's not trendy.............allegedly!

Craig Revel Horwood who hails from down under
Danced in musicals by Andrew Lloyd Webber
In Strictly Come Dancing
Contestants were smarting
As he's a critical choreographer!

Busty, giggly actress from Shoreditch
One-take Windsor, born Barbara-Ann Deeks,
She Carried On with Sid James
Then to Albert Square she came
To be matriarch of the Queen Vic!

Two real estate moguls from London
For Kirstie and Phil the search is on
Don your scarf and flatties
For viewing properties
Location, Location, Location!

A comedy duo from Newcastle
Byker Grovers presented Pop Idol,
I'm a Celebrity,
Saturday Night Takeaway
Ant and Dec "Let's get ready to Rhumble!"

PROMINENT POLITICIANS

Gordon Brown, the MP for Dunfermline,
As Chancellor thought spending was a sin
No more Tory boom and bust
In his prudence we trust
As PM "Let the work of change begin!"

Born and raised in Glasgow, Menzies Campbell, QC
Olympic Veteran, Menzies Campbell, CBE
The Lib Dem leader
Now lives in Cupar
Representing Fife North East, Menzies Campbell, MP!

A Labour man born in Edinburgh
Tony Blair, destined for Prime Minister
His legacy of war
Was not worth fighting for
Bush's puppet, or just an Ugly Rumour?

Raised in Midland and Houston in Texas
Owned a company into oil and gas
From Texas Government
To US President
Waged war on Terror, George Dubya Bush!

Born in Grantham, a greengrocer's daughter
The first UK woman Prime Minister
So said the Iron Lady
"Every PM needs a Willie"
She's not for turning, she's Maggie Thatcher!

Prezza, born Prestatyn, good for gags
Protecting Pauline's hair-do with Two Jags
Ex-waiter Merchant Navy
No Jobs, PM's Deputy
Left with egg on his face, threw Two Jabs!

From Clay Cross, MP Dennis Skinner
Ex-miner and Labour backbencher
"Marvellous Parliamentarian"
And low expense claimant
On the Awkward Squad Bench, Beast of Bolsover!

Socialist born in the Lambeth borough
Red Ken became the GLC leader
Brent Cross Labour MP
Expelled from the Party
But back in again now he's London's Mayor!

Tory Party leader born in London
Privileged education at Eton
He is the MP
For Oxon's Witney
He wants to switch on a whole new generation!

Born in New York, educated at Eton
Alexander Boris de Pfeffel Johnson
Henley Tory MP
Eccentric and scatty
Made to say sorry to Liverpudlians!

William Jefferson Bligh, number III
Loves to play sax, married Hilary
Has a law degree from Yale
He smoked, but didn't inhale
Please don't mention Monica Lewinsky!

POPULAR PRESENTERS

From Romford in Essex, Richard Madeley
Was a presenter on daytime telly
His Ali G impression
Was comedy from heaven
But nothing on his couch romp with Shakey!

Born in Manchester, up north, Judy Finnigan
Was a presenter on the te-le-vis-i-on
At an awards ceremony
Broadcast on national TV
Her boobs came out, John Leslie put them in again!

Born in London, Streetmate Davina
Famous Big Brother presenter
From singing waitress
To The Brits hostess
Please do not say f**k or bu**er!

Bearded ex-Radio One DJ
Went from Swap Shop to Noel's House Party
His now famous schpeel
"Deal or No Deal"
Should be gunged for creating Mr Blobby!

First lady of GMTV
She's Rector of Dundee Uni
Walk off the Pounds
Go Figure It Out
She's that lovely Lorraine Kelly!

A man on the telly from Oldham
Going Live, Phillip Schofield showed 'em
Left Gordon the Gopher
For Joseph in Technicolour
Onto double entendres with Fern Britton!

An all round entertainer born in Stepney
Morecambe and Wise mocked his singing ability
The new Countdown presenter
Evergreen Des O'Connor
A new dad despite being over seventy!

Born in Leeds, Jeremy Paxman
University Challenge frontman
His Newsnight questioning
Howard not answering
"Did you threaten to overrule him?"

Carol Vorderman raised in North Wales
Started work in electrical sales
Does her sums on Countdown
Detoxed her weight down
High IQ crumpet for all the males!

A Yorkshire man from Cudworth, Barnsley
Definitive chat show host, Parkie
Wrestled by Rod Hull's Emu
Dreadful Meg Ryan interview
Done them all from Tom Cruise to Ali!

A radio presenter born in Edinburgh
Went from One to 5 live to work with Shelagh
The Wheel of Fortune's spinning
Rest of His Life Watchdogging
Nicky Campbell, Who Do You Think You Are?

Born in Limerick, young Terry Wogan
The Eurovision Song Contest man
He showed us Auntie's Bloomers
And he's the record holder
Of the longest golf putt shown on television!

DJ Chris Evans born in Warrington
Did the breakfast show on Radio One
Don't Forget your Toothbrush
After your Big Breakfast
What will be the next Ginger Production?

Chris Tarrant born in Reading, Berkshire
Ex lorry driver and school teacher
On Tiswas he sang along
With The Bucket of Water song
So, Who Wants to be a Millionaire?

A presenter born in Ealing in London
Teamed with Fred Dineage and that Nick Owen
Married chef Phil Vickery
But eats Ryvita Minis
Now giggling with Phil Schofield, it's Fern Britton!

Chat show host born in Leytonstone, London
Film buff took over from Barry Norman
Talk show on the wadio
Four Poofs and a Piano
It's Friday Night with Woss, Jonathan!

ENTERTAINING ENTREPRENEURS

An entrepreneur born in Hackney
Founder of the Amstrad Company
Well known philanthropist
Star of The Apprentice
Fired them all, but not dreaded Katie!

From Queens, head of Organizations Trump
Tower, Plaza, Casinos - all named Trump
Owns Universe, Miss
Hired The Apprentice
Now Donald's into fragrance – 'Eau de Trump'?

A Tycoon residing in Surrey
When young ran a tennis academy
Peter Jones of Dragons' Den
Is worth two hundred million
He knows how to lose and make money!

Born in Bakos, famous Egyptian
A billionaire and businessman
Owner of Harrods, Knightsbridge
Chairman at Craven Cottage
But can't get a passport from Britain!

Self-made millionaire born in Limassol
Theo Paphitis, the Lion of Millwall
Took over Contessa
Now into La Senza
In ladies' undies he's having a ball!

From Clydebank, a Scottish Businessman
Duncan Bannatyne, a TV Dragon
Discharged from the Navy
Received an OBE
He started with an ice cream van in Stockton!

CELEBRITY CHEFS

Australasian chef, loves organic food
He's the MasterChef Going Large dude
He judges along with Greg
The guru of fruit and veg
But have you got the passion, John Torode?

Brought up near Castle Howard in Yorkshire
Scarborough Tech's three times student of the year
Sweet Baby James Martin
He took to his dancin'
But did Camilla and he make a pair?

There once was a feckin' chef from Johnstone
Whose feckin' name was Ramsay, Gordon
As hard as he might try
To eat his Humble Pie
He had lots of feckin' stars Michelin!

A charismatic chef born in Balham
Ainsley Harriott's heritage is Jamaican
His flamboyance took
Him to Ready Steady Cook
Aboard the Gourmet Express to Clapham!

A television chef born in Woking
Delia wrote How to Cheat at Cooking
Canaries' director
And cuisine instructor
Half time, "Let's be 'aving you!" she's shouting!

A queen of the kitchen, born in London
Domestic Goddess, Nigella Lawson
Spectator food writer
Charles Saatchi's her partner
Nigella Bites on the television!

A great French chef from Besançon
Owns Le Manoir aux Quat'Saisons
Wrote Foolproof French Cookery
Now reality TV
Slow-mo food fights in The Restaurant!

From Essex young cook Jamie Oliver
Naked Chef and taste bud trouble shooter
Espoused proper nutrition
For those in education
He said "These turkey twizzlers ain't pukka!"

A man born in Stratford-on-Avon
Was named Antony Worrall Thompson
Started 'Menage à Trois'
But made a faux pas
In the jungle, led a food rebellion!

FAMOUS FOR BEING FAMOUS

Kerry Katona from Warrington, Cheshire
Won I'm a Celebrity Get Me Out of Here!
Pregnant by Brian McFadden
She left Atomic Kitten
Now voted Celebrity Mum of the Year!

From New York, Paris, Hilton heiress
Socialite of magnitude, Princess
No Simple Life, she's hot!
So's Tinkerbell the dog
Can't pay to have her big feet made less!

From Essex, Brian Belo off Big Brother
Fancied pink twin Amanda, not Samantha
Well, who was Shakespeare?
He has no idea!
"Shut Up!" 'cos he's one hundred grand richer!

Tara Palmer-Tomkinson from Dummer
Famous It girl, royal skiing partner
She won Fame Academy
But rehab's the place to be
After being on the show of Frank Skinner!

Born in San Jose, son of George, Calum Best
Put Celebrity Love Island to the test
The first time with Rebecca
Then won it with Bianca
Now he's trying to fit in all the rest!

From Essex Wives, she's Keeping It Real
Exposing her flesh - no big deal
More a belt than a skirt
Tabloids dig up the dirt
Jodie Marsh: Who Will Take Her Up the Aisle?

A dental nurse who came from Bermondsey
"East Angular's abroad" said Jade Goody
Her Big Brother fame
Meant financial gain
But she had to close her salon, Uglys!

A top glamour model from Brighton
Katie Price, better known as Jordan,
Jungle celebrity
Married Peter Andre
Now writing, but famous for big ones!

SUPERLATIVE SPORTSPEOPLE

A masticating football legend from Govan
Man United Manager, Alex Ferguson
Won the treble, yes, all three
Won't speak to the BBC
Punched below the waist by a Scot at Euston!

Freddie Flintoff from Preston, Lancashire
Won Sports Personality of the Year
Named Man of the Series
Against the West Indies
So why sail a pedalo and drink beer?

There was an Everton fan born in Chester
Michael Owen, Liverpool's top goal scorer
Left Anfield for Real
Madrid for Newcastle
Famed for the wonder goal against Argentina!

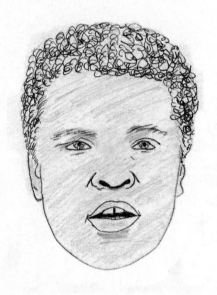

A boxer born in Louisville, Kentucky
Cassius Clay became Muhammad Ali
He beat the very best
Was known as The Greatest
"Floats like a butterfly and stings like a bee!"

A talented striker from Leicester
Christened Gary Winston Lineker
Always first in the box
Never ever sent off
True to his goals, he didn't Quaver!

Star rugby player from Frimley, Surrey,
Had an arm, knee and shoulder injury
Club team Newcastle Falcons
Played with the British Lions
Scored winning drop goal World Cup 2003!

Born in Stevenage, Lewis Hamilton
After karting signed up with McClaren
Alonso's down in the dumps
Spent too long at the pumps
Who should be the next F1 Champion?

A footballer born in Lancashire
Sir Geoff Hurst, England's World Cup striker
Back in Sixty-six
That famous hat trick
"Crowd on the pitch, they think it's all over
.........it is now!"

A man born in Upper Ferntree Gully
Taken the most Test wickets in history
Superlative bowling
Known for his sledging
"Bowled Shane! Keep your hair on, Warney!"

From a boxing family in Liverpool
Teenage Wayne Rooney scored goal after goal
Went out with Coleen McLoughlin
Moved to Man U from Everton
Sent off against Portugal - played the wrong ball!

A tennis player born in Weston on the Green
For Tim Henman winning Wimbledon was the dream
He saw off Greg Ruzedski
And now there's Andy Murray
But "Come on Tim" still echoes in SW19!

A football legend born in Três Corações
Pelé wore the number 10 shirt for Santos
Four World Cup campaigns
In Brazil he reigns
As his hat trick world record shows his greatness!

A rugby player from Bridgend, Cymru
He plays for the Ospreys in Swansea
His name's Gavin Henson
He's too vain to mention
Out of the World Cup due to injury!

There was a footballing Swede from Torsby
Came over to England from Italy
Sven-Göran Eriksson
As the national coach done
Moving up in the world to Man City!

There was a man from Cypress, California
Named Eldrick Woods, commonly known as Tiger
He always wears red
Knocks his putts stone dead
Birdied or bogied, he's the world's top golfer!

Born in Northwich, Ms Radcliffe, known as Paula
England's superlative marathon runner
Olympic gold dream
Cut off in midstream
Despite relieving herself in the gutter!

José Mourinho born in Setúbal
Top manager of Porto, Portugal
Tiff with Roman Abramovitch
So he left Stamford Bridge
Where will he go, the one who is special?

A man born in Leytonstone, London
Top midfielder, fashion and style icon.
He made lots of dosh
Got married to Posh
Adios Madrid, to L.A. he's gone!

KINGS OF COMEDY

A Grays man, writer in the Guardian
Voted Sexiest Vegetarian
Big Mouth of Big Brother
Russell Brand, no other
Sacked for dressing up as Osama Bin Laden!

Famous funny Brummie, Jasper Carrott
Rode his Funky Moped on the Magic Roundabout
Enough Carrott's Lib
And The Detectives
Not ginger, but Golden Balls, no doubt!

Ricky Gervais born in Reading
The singer in Seona Dancing
Left his Office pals
To write Flanimals
But we want to see David Brent dancing!

A dead-pan humorist born in London
He's a comedian's comedian
Room 101 cast away
Whose Line is it Anyway?
Have I Got News for You, Paul Merton?

A comedian born in Birkenhead
Taught by the Christian Brothers, it is said
Before Buster and Olga
Lily Savage persona
Won a Blankety Blank cheque book and pen!

STARS OF THE SILVER SCREEN

From New Jersey, Disco King, John Travolta
Strutting his stuff in Saturday Night Fever
From Tony Manero
Greased as Danny Zuko
Look Who's Talking as Cool as Chili Palmer!

An actor of note, born Mount Vernon
To a minister and a beautician
Played Malcolm X for Spike Lee
And Steve Biko for Dickie
Cry Freedom, it's Denzel Washington!

An actor born in Shawnee, Oklahoma
Starred in films containing many a number
From Twelve Monkeys to Se7en
And to Ocean's Eleven
Brad Pitt moved on from Jen to Angelina!

Renée Zellweger from Texas, Katy
Won an Oscar as Cold Mountain's Ruby
Classic line we all know
"You had me at Hello"
Gained twenty pounds for Bridget Jones's Diary!

For a man born in New York, Syracuse
Acting was a Risky Business to choose
Born on the Fourth of July
The Last Samurai
There's no Mission Impossible for Tom Cruise!

A Kentish actor from Canterbury
Orlando Bloom was in Casualty
and Extras. For Troy, he stood
As Legolas of Mirkwood
Accused fellow actors of Elf-envy!

Regal actress, Dame Helen Mirren, from London
Her royal portrayal meant an Oscar was won
For The Queen, Britain's figurehead
But as a Calendar Girl said
"We're going to need considerably bigger buns!"

There was an actress from Reading in Berkshire
Named Kate Winslet, a Heavenly Creature.
Sense and Sensibility
Not at all Hideous Kinky
Nominated four times for an Oscar!

Enigmatic actor born in Owensboro
Nightmare on Elm Street to Sleepy Hollow
Edward Scissorhands
Found his Neverland
But he's best known as Captain Jack Sparrow!

An actor from Lewisham, London
In Cold Mountain Jude Law played Inman
Mr Ripley's Dickie
Oscar Wilde's Lord Bosie
But only two Oscar nominations!

A big-footed actress from Boston
Uma made a Dangerous Liaison
Tarantino's muse
Got nothing to lose
Dancing with Travolta in Pulp Fiction!

Teenage heart-throb from Hollywood, California
Dramatised OCD in The Aviator
Leo DiCaprio
More Jack than Romeo
Catch Him if You Can, as Frank Abagnale Junior!

An actor from Lexington, Kentucky
Became known as "Gorgeous George" Clooney
Good Night, Doctor Ross
Good Luck, Captain Bosche
Out of Sight Intolerable Cruelty!

There was a Shakespearian actress from Yorkshire
Whose eight minute performance won her an Oscar
Judi Dench was her name
The Queen made her a Dame
Despite flirting with Mr Brown as Queen Victoria!

Born in Melbourne, Australia, star of Babel
Seduced a schoolboy in Notes on Scandal
As an actress, Cate Blanchett,
Definitely has The Gift
And her pointed ears from playing Elf Queen, Galadriel!

An actor born in Cambridge, Massachusetts
Wrote Good Will Hunting with his mate, Ben Affleck
Talented Mr Ripley
Shunned his Bourne Identity
Will Jason Bourne resurface? Place your bets!

Born in New York, Robert De Niro Junior
Was Untouchable playing Taxi Driver
Oscar won for Raging
Bull, his method acting
Meant gaining fifty pounds for Jake La Motta!

From New York, Alfredo James Pacino
Played Corleone, Brasco - Mafioso
And The Merchant of Venice
But he also played police
In Heat, Sea of Love and in Serpico!

There was a beautiful actress from Teddington
As Jules Paxton tried to Bend it Like Beckham
Without Prejudice as Lizzie
Nor Pride, Keira Knightley
Swashbuckled in Pirates of the Caribbean!

REAL ROYALTY

Her Majesty the Queen born in London
Married Lieutenant Philip Mountbatten
Famed Tupperware server
And Corgi dog lover
Don't want another annus horriblis to happen!

Prince Philip of Greece and Denmark, it's told
Left Corfu for France as a one-year old
He studied at Gordonstoun
As 'The Duke of Gaffes' he's known
Has put his foot in it all over the world!

Born in London, Anne, The Princess Royal
In the Olympic team at Montreal
Although ill at ease
Works for charities
Prosecuted – can't control her dog at all!

The Queen's heir born at Buckingham Palace
Hates carbuncles, but shows no malice
A Royal Navy Captain
A massive Goons Show fan
Is the Crown of England a poisoned chalice?

Fourth in line, Prince Andrew, Duke of York
Made headlines going out with Koo Stark
Served in the Royal Navy
And then he married Fergie
Divorced now, but she made her mark!

From London, Earl of Wessex, Prince Edward
The Cambridge Grad found army life no good
Did It's a Royal Knockout
The media made him shout
His acting was so little understood!

Prince William who was born in Paddington
Was educated near Windsor, at Eton
Went to St Andrew's Uni
And the Sandhurst Academy
But will his future be with Kate Middleton?

Young Prince born at St Mary's hospital
Harry was christened at Windsor Castle
Works hard for charity
But he likes to party
His fancy dress blunder was awful!

ALPHABETICAL INDEX

Look out for Helen M. Grant's
next title

"Sporting Limericks"

ISBN 978-1-906375-01-0

If you would like to write to Helen M. Grant,
please e-mail:
helengrant@overtheramparts.co.uk

Over the Ramparts Publishing

"Books with a difference"

To find out about forthcoming titles, please visit
our website

www.overtheramparts.co.uk